A Guide for Using

To Kill a Mockingbird

in the Classroom

Based on the novel written by Harper Lee

*This guide written by **Mari Lu Robbins, M.A.***

Teacher Created Resources, Inc.
6421 Industry Way
Westminster, CA 92683
www.teachercreated.com
ISBN: 978-1-57690-626-2
©*1999 Teacher Created Resources, Inc.*
Reprinted, 2008
Made in U.S.A.

Edited by
Dona Herweck Rice

Illustrated by
Blanca Apodaca

Cover Art by
Blanca Apodaca

Table of Contents

Introduction

Good literature never dies; it just gets better with age. *To Kill a Mockingbird* has everything a reader could want in a book: wonderful characters, an engaging plot, and inspirational and transforming ideas. Over and over we can turn to it for enjoyment, saying each time we do, "Oh, I never read it that way before! How wonderful!"

In *Literature Units*, great care has been taken to select pieces of literature which the reader can come to appreciate and enjoy.

Teachers who use this unit will find the following features to supplement their own valuable ideas:

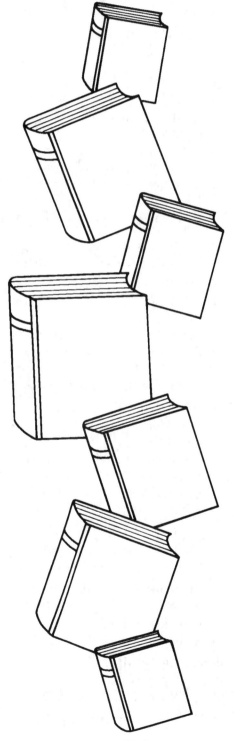

- Sample Lesson Plans

- Pre-reading Activities

- Biographical Sketch of the Author

- Book Summary

- Vocabulary Lists and Activities

- Chapters grouped for study with activities including the following:

    —a quiz

    —a hands-on project

    —a cooperative learning activity

    —a cross-curricular connection

    —an extension into the reader's life

- Post-reading Activities

- Book Report Ideas

- Research Ideas

- A Culminating Activity

- Three Unit Test Options

- A Bibliography of Related Reading

- An Answer Key

We are certain that this unit will be a worthwhile addition to your planning, and we hope that as you use our ideas, your students will increase their appreciation of good literature.

Sample Lesson Plans

Each lesson suggested below may take from one to several days to complete.

Lesson 1

- Introduce and complete some or all of the pre-reading activities found on page 5.
- Read "About the Author" with your students (page 6).
- Read the book summary with your students (page 7).
- Introduce the vocabulary list for Section 1 (page 8).

Lesson 2

- Read Section 1 of the novel. As you read, place the vocabulary words (page 8) in the context of the story and discuss their meanings.
- Complete a vocabulary activity (page 9).
- Complete "Anticipation Guide" (page 11).
- Learn about myths (pages 12 and 13).
- Learn about "The Great Depression" (pages 14 and 15).
- Begin "Reading Response Journals" (page 16).
- Administer the Section 1 quiz (page 10).
- Introduce the vocabulary list for Section 2 (page 8).

Lesson 3

- Read Section 2. Place the vocabulary words (page 8) in context and discuss their meanings.
- Complete a vocabulary activity (page 9).
- Complete "Who-Am-I Collages" (page 18).
- Learn about "Idioms" (page 19).
- Learn about rabies (page 20).
- Role-play the suggested situations (page 21).
- Administer the Section 2 quiz (page 17).
- Introduce the vocabulary list for Section 3 (page 8).

Lesson 4

- Read Section 3. Place the vocabulary words (page 8) in context and discuss their meanings.
- Complete a vocabulary activity (page 9).
- Learn about "Southern Cooking" (page 23).
- Learn about being a southern lady (page 24).
- Learn about "Similes and Metaphors" (page 25).
- Learn about "Allusions" (page 26).
- Administer the Section 3 quiz (page 22).
- Introduce the vocabulary list for Section 4 (page 8).

Lesson 5

- Read Section 4. Place the vocabulary words (page 8) in context and discuss their meanings.
- Complete a vocabulary activity (page 9).
- Construct a "Characterization Chart" (page 28).
- Learn about "Setting" (page 29).
- Analyze a character (page 30).
- Discuss "Adult Conversations" (page 31).
- Administer the Section 4 quiz (page 27).
- Introduce the vocabulary words (page 8) for Section 5.

Lesson 6

- Read Section 5. Place the vocabulary words (page 8) in context and discuss their meanings.
- Compete a vocabulary activity (page 9).
- Make a "Bookworm" (page 33).
- Learn about "Themes" (page 34).
- Learn about "Racial Hatred and Discrimination" (page 35).
- Construct a diary for Boo (page 36).
- Administer the Section 5 quiz (page 32).

Lesson 7

- Discuss questions your students may have about the book (page 40).
- Assign book report and research projects (pages 41 and 42).
- Begin work on the "Culminating Activity" (page 43).

Lesson 8

- Administer one or more unit tests (pages 44, 45, and 46).
- Discuss the students' opinions and enjoyment of the book.
- Provide a list of related reading for the students (page 47).

Lesson 9

- Hold the "Culminating Activity" (page 43).

4

Before the Book

Teaching *To Kill a Mockingbird* can be a marvelous experience for you and your students. It is one of those rare books which captures the very essence of a time and place in American life which no longer exists in its entirety, but which has had tremendous impact on the present day. It was a time of contradictions: love and hate, prosperity and dire poverty, celebrated freedom and rank injustice. This book provides an opportunity for the teacher to explore and discuss some of these problems which have remained throughout the decades since the book's setting.

Preparing students for the content of *To Kill a Mockingbird* is crucial to their full understanding of the book, as well as to their ability to recognize some of the social problems in the United States centering around racial attitudes. Dealing with the issues in the book can be a powerful way to help heal the wounds that generate racial divisions still present in our society. Try one or more of the following activities.

1. Explore the impact of the Great Depression on America in the 1930s. Today's students may have no conception of the widespread poverty and ignorance which existed during this time when millions of people were out of work nor the impact this had on the ideas and beliefs of the poor who were most affected. The bibliography includes resources and Internet sites where students can see for themselves how poverty distorted life views and values. This might be a good time to show the films *The Grapes of Wrath* and *Of Mice and Men* which provide graphic coverage of what life was like for millions of people.

2. The language of the novel must be addressed. The word "nigger" is inflammatory, but it was in common usage during the time of the novel. It must be brought into the open and looked at honestly. This will be an especially sensitive subject in a racially-mixed classroom. Students need to understand the difference between the word's definition and its connotative meaning and how those go together negatively to define a group of people. Inform students that during the reading of the book they will be asked to identify the different ways "nigger" is used by different people in the book and why that is important. Always remember that some students and parents will feel pain at the very utterance of the word, so outside the reading of the book, the term "non-white" may be a better term to use during discussion. Do not allow any student to be teased or ridiculed by classmates because of the word.

3. Is justice truly blind? In America, the idea of justice is sometimes treated as if a democracy automatically ensures it. Discuss the following questions with the students.

   • In real life, does one person always receive the same treatment as another?

   • What causes differences between one person's justice and another's injustice?

   • What, indeed, is "justice"?

   • Does justice apply equally to the rich and the poor? to the white and the non-white? to the socially prominent and the social outcast? to the male and the female? to the adult and the child?

   • Where do we draw our lines concerning with whom we deal justly and with whom we do not?

   • Should we change the way our society deals with all citizens?

   • Tell students they will be reading about a man who tries to change things. After reading the book, ask them if he is in any way successful.

About the Author

Nelle Harper Lee decided she wanted to be a writer when she was seven years old, growing up in Monroeville, Alabama. Her childhood was very much like Scout's in *To Kill a Mockingbird*, and she knew of many cases in which black men were unjustly convicted and imprisoned or executed for raping white women. Her father was a lawyer, and for a time she was sidetracked into the study of law at the University of Alabama. She also attended Oxford University in England as an exchange student for one year, but she found she did not want to be a lawyer after all—she wanted to write. She quit her law studies and her job as an airlines reservations clerk and moved into a tiny cold-water apartment in New York City, which she furnished with castoffs and orange crates. There she began her writing career.

When she took her first stories to an agent, the agent liked one of them and encouraged her to expand it into a novel. At about this time, Lee's father, Amasa Lee, became ill, and she began traveling frequently to Alabama. During these visits to Monroeville, Lee was once again confronted with the scenes and people of her childhood, one of whom had been her childhood friend, Truman Capote, who would become the model for the character of Dill in her book. She found a fertile field in which to sow her literary seeds in the lush environs of Alabama, and she began working on *To Kill a Mockingbird*.

She finished her first draft of the novel in 1957, but the first editor to read it turned it down, so she spent another two and one-half years rewriting and revising what she had begun. It was difficult and discouraging at times, writing the book over and over again, but she did not give up until she finally got it the way she wanted it. When it was published in 1960, her hard work was rewarded. Critics loved the book, and readers of all ages agreed. It became a selection for several book clubs, and the movie rights were sold almost immediately. The film, starring Gregory Peck as Atticus Finch, is one of the few movie gems in which the essence of a novel is captured on film. In 1961, Lee was awarded the Pulitzer Prize for Fiction.

Harper Lee was suddenly famous. Stories about her appeared in all the leading magazines and newspapers. Lee, basically a private person who did not relish being the object of attention, soon acquired the reputation of being a recluse, which she was not. When interviewers asked her whether she was writing another novel, she said she was, but that novel has never been published.

Harper Lee has, over the years, become almost a mythical literary figure, even though she has never published another book. She is not a hermit. According to friends and relatives, she is a jolly and genial person, but she still enjoys her privacy and spends equal amounts of time between New York City and her hometown of Monroeville. According to a story by Kathy Kemp in *The News Observer* (November 12, 1997), Lee's cousin says she once told him when he asked why she had never written another book, "When you have a hit like that, you can't go anywhere but down."

To Kill a Mockingbird

by Harper Lee

(Warner Books, Inc., 1960, 1982)

(available in CAN, UK, & AUS from Warner Books, Inc.)

Jean Louise Finch, called Scout by her family, is six, and her brother Jem is ten when *To Kill a Mockingbird* begins. Set in the small town of Maycomb, Alabama, during the Great Depression days of the 1930s, the novel opens during summer. When Scout begins telling her story, she and Jem meet a new playmate, Dill, who has come to spend the summer with his aunt. Dill is a curious and mischievous child, fascinated by tales he hears of "Boo" Radley, the neighborhood recluse who unwittingly generates much conjecture about who he is and what he is like because no one has seen him for years. The children spend their summer devising games intended to get Boo to come out, but they have no success.

When school begins, Scout is disappointed. She learns her teacher is horrified that Scout can already read. Scout longs for summer to return so that she, Jem, and Dill can try again to see Boo Radley. The children begin finding small gifts—an old watch, some chewing gum, and other small things—left in the knothole of a tree on the corner of the Radley property.

When Dill returns the following summer, the children once again scheme to bring out Boo, but slowly they begin to realize Boo is not the monster they had imagined. They also discover that the gifts were left for them by Boo himself.

Meanwhile, the Finch children fear that their lawyer father, Atticus, is a coward because he does not like guns as do the other men in the county. Then they see him shoot a mad dog with one shot. They are confused when children begin calling Atticus "nigger lover" because he is defending a poor black man, Tom Robinson, accused of raping a poor, ignorant, white woman named Mayella Ewell. Atticus knows Tom is innocent, and despite the namecalling and intimidation from whites who think he should not try to get Tom acquitted of the crime, Atticus gives Tom his best defense as the children watch the trial from the "colored" balcony.

Atticus's efforts on Tom's behalf are to no avail due to the place and time period of the trial, and Tom attempts to escape prison. In doing so, he is shot to death. Scout, Jem, and Dill learn difficult lessons about the nature of injustice. In their time and place, the word of a despicable white man is taken against that of a hard-working, honest, and good-hearted black man, and even the best efforts of a gifted lawyer are not enough to save him.

However, the story does not end there. Scout, herself, is then placed in danger by the victorious and vicious white man who wants revenge on Atticus for showing him to be the truly evil person he is. Only the heroism of the least likely person in Maycomb saves Scout from being killed, and Scout learns the real meaning of courage, understanding, and tolerance.

In *To Kill a Mockingbird*, Harper Lee has created unforgettable characters and illustrated a time and place which will always be associated with this book. It has never been out of print since its first printing, and in 1995 it was re-released in a new, hardback, thirty-fifth anniversary issue. This truly is a book the reader can turn to again and again, gaining new insights and knowledge each time. It is one of a kind, and the reader is richer indeed for having read it.

Vocabulary Lists

Here are vocabulary lists that correspond to each section of the book, as outlined in the table of contents (page 2). Vocabulary activity ideas can be found on the next page.

Section 1

synonyms	collards	repertoire
malevolent	predilection	beadle
inquisitive	benign	dispensation
erratic	iniquities	contentious
monosyllabic	Gothic	probate
edification	cowlick	vapid
nocturnal	domiciled	nebulous
indigenous	meditating	condescended
tranquility	benevolence	diminutive
auspicious	melancholy	magisterial

Section 2

commotion	caricature	essence
articulate	perplexity	ingenuous
puny	passé	trousseau
inordinate	innate	undulate
changeling	ascertaining	meteorological
malignant	morphodite	Confederate
mortify	apoplectic	analogous
oppressive	compensation	gravitate
lineament	viscous	
hookah	rudiment	
palliation	deportment	

Section 3

appalling	altercation	elucidate
habiliment	uncouth	ecclesiastic
impedimenta	ambidextrous	corset
fey	myopic	speculate
elusive	acrimonious	placid
inconsistent	bode	acquiescence
rotogravure	qualms	contemptuous
congenial	tedious	prerogative
obliquely	caste	preoccupation
resignation	infallible	venerable

Section 4

irrelevant	perpetual	yonder
involuntary	duress	scrutiny
instinctive	humidity	expunge
impudent	corroborative	distaff
temerity	cynical	acquittal
immaterial	neutrality	pilgrimage
arid	browbeat	exodus
volition	ex cathedra	sibilant
perpetrate	contraband	unmitigated
integrity	credibility	vehement

Section 5

remorse	garish	pinion
clarify	spurious	turmoil
apprehension	savor	muse
ascertain	squander	purloin
perforate	mortification	ghoul
recluse	competent	mantelpiece
notoriety	dynamic	conceive (of)
incantation	eccentricity	
lichen	divinity	

8

Vocabulary Activities

Completing a variety of activities with the vocabulary words will enable students to become familiar with the words and to use them in everyday speech. Here are a few ideas to try.

Word-a-Day: Each day students choose an unfamiliar word from the sectional list. They find and record all the definitions given of the word and then find the word in the novel by skimming through the section, deciding which definition fits the way it is used there. They record any interesting history the word has and write a sentence using the word. After discussing the word, they place information they have collected about the word into a vocabulary archive. After reading the novel, they put the words they have collected into a class dictionary which they illustrate and put on display as part of the culminating activities for the book's study.

Definition Bee: Students are grouped into teams. Alternating sides, either the teacher or a monitor reads the definition of a word for a student, and the student identifies the word being defined. As a word is identified, the side whose member identifies it gets a point. The first side to amass a given number of points is declared the winner.

Play Twenty Clues: In this game a student gives clues about a vocabulary word, and the other students have twenty chances to identify the word. The student who correctly identifies the word gives the next set of clues.

Parts-of-Speech Chart: Students make a chart with headings such as Noun, Verb, Adjective, and Adverb. Under the appropriate heading, have them write each word in the context of a sentence, correctly showing its use in that part of speech.

Word Puzzles: Have students make crossword or word-search puzzles, using vocabulary words. The puzzles may be duplicated to share with the entire class.

Riddles: Write riddles using vocabulary words. For example, "What's green and nutritious and goes with fatback?" The answer is "collards."

Sentence Blanks: Provide sentences, each containing a blank where a vocabulary word belongs. Have students use context clues to fill in the blanks with the correct vocabulary words.

Internet Vocabulary Trips: Here are some Internet sites where students can find information about the words in the vocabulary lists and about other words in which they are interested.

> **The Logical World of Etymology:** *http://www.phoenix.net/~melanie/arc_*
>
> **Word for Word:** *http://www.peg.apc.org/~toconnor/welcome.html*
>
> **WWWebster Dictionary:** *http://www.m-w.com/dictionary*
>
> **Online Dictionaries, Glossaries and Encyclopedias:**
> *http://www-ocean.tamu.edu/~baum/hyperref.html*

Quiz Time!

1. List three important events from this section.

   _____

   _____

   _____

   _____

   _____

2. List details which establish the setting of *To Kill a Mockingbird*.

   _____

   _____

3. Who are Scout and Jem's parents?

   _____

   _____

4. List at least three details which describe Dill.

   _____

   _____

5. Why does Scout describe Walter Cunningham's life situation to her teacher?

   _____

   _____

6. What do Jem and Scout think of the things they find in the knothole of the tree?

   _____

   _____

7. Why do the people of Maycomb dislike the Radleys?

   _____

   _____

8. What's a "hot steam?" _____

   _____

9. Who is Miss Maudie? _____

   _____

10. On the back of this page, tell how Dill and Scout's lives are different from one another. Include details.

Anticipation Guide

To Kill a Mockingbird is an evocative and powerful novel. Your students will enjoy and understand it better if they prepare to read it by considering some of the questions and issues within it, especially since the story, the characters, and the setting have implications for present-day life which your students may not think of on their own. As with any story, prior knowledge of certain basic concepts, including human behaviors and beliefs, is crucial to your students' full comprehension. It may also benefit everyone to relate the people and events in the book to those in their own lives.

Before the students begin reading the book, ask them to give their thoughtful opinions in response to the "Anticipation Guide" statements below. Explain that there are no right or wrong answers and that they will not be graded on their responses. After the students have completed the guide, discuss their answers and the reasons they gave them. After reading the book, have the students respond again to the same statements. Discuss if and how their opinions have changed. Return both guides to the students and have them compare their own answers.

Respond to each of the following statements with *agree* or *disagree*.

_____ 1. In America, everyone has the same chance to succeed as everyone else.

_____ 2. A hero is someone who succeeds at whatever he or she sets out to do.

_____ 3. Majority rule is the best way because most people do what is right.

_____ 4. A model family consists of a father, a mother, and children.

_____ 5. Girls should act like girls, and boys should act like boys.

_____ 6. In America, we all know that a person is innocent of a crime until proven guilty in a court of law. If he or she is judged guilty, we know it is true.

_____ 7. You can usually tell what kind of person someone is by how he or she looks.

_____ 8. If someone stays away from people, he or she probably has something to hide.

_____ 9. Some words are so offensive they should never be said or written.

_____ 10. Sticks and stones may break your bones, but words will never hurt you.

Myths and Urban Myths

Myths are not just stories people believed long ago. People throughout time have believed myths. The people of Maycomb County in the 1930s did, and we have myths we believe today. Myths help us make sense of our world. They explain why things are the way we think they are, why people do as they do. Myths are not always about gods and goddesses. They explain the trivial as well as the important. They may not be true, but many people believe them anyway.

The myths of Maycomb County taught its citizens that certain things were true: Crawfords don't mind their own business; Bufords walk a certain way because they're Bufords; Delafields don't tell the truth, so never take a check from one without calling the bank first; Mrs. Merriweather sips gin out of a Lydia Pinkham tonic bottle just like her mother did; non-whites are not quite human and do not fall under the same protection as whites; a lazy white man is more deserving of justice than a hard-working non-white.

While Scout, Jem, and Dill, thanks to the admonitions of Atticus, do not believe the local myths about non-whites, they have their own myths. Many of these concern Arthur "Boo" Radley, who is white. Since they have never seen him, despite his living nearby, they speculate about him endlessly. They think that he goes out at night when it is pitch dark to spy through folks' windows and to scratch at their screens; that he is six-and-one-half feet tall and eats raw squirrels and cats, leaving his hands bloodstained; that his face is scarred, his teeth yellow, his eyes popped out, and he drools. One could be killed just going up to his door and knocking!

Their myths about Boo lead the children into mischief. They become obsessed with the prospect of making Boo "come out," while at the same time they fear doing so. Their summers center around an irresistible desire to see Boo in the flesh, while at the same time they dread the terrible fate which awaits them if they do. It feels to them like walking barefoot down a grassy path, hoping to see a rattlesnake in the grass but fearing getting bitten while doing so.

In the meantime, while the children's self-made explanations about Boo Radley color their days and lead them into less than compassionate activities aimed at seeing him, the townspeople's explanations about non-whites and whites lead them to accept activities aimed at preserving life as they have always known it. Their myths tell them things should stay the way they have always been to make the world safer. Then they suddenly learn to their shame that what they had always known to be true may not be true after all.

What kinds of myths do we have today? Most are harmless, the stuff of entertainment. Some are beliefs which lead people to fear and illogical behaviors.

Our modern world is filled with a new phenomenon called the urban myth or legend. These are stories and beliefs which get started in various ways. Sometimes a television personality makes an offhand statement which is taken seriously. A talk-show host may state an opinion his or her listeners take as gospel truth. Someone posts something on the Internet on a message board which is repeated and spread onto other boards and other venues until no one knows where it began. A newspaper editor writes an opinion which is taken as fact. Sometimes an urban myth gets started as a joke which, over time, is taken seriously.

On the following page are some urban myths and their possible origins. Read them and then do the activities that follow.

Myths and Urban Myths (cont.)

Here are some recent urban myths and their possible explanations.

1. **Urban Myth:** A thriving colony of white alligators lives in the sewers of New York City, the offspring of baby alligators brought back as pets from Florida, where they grow to huge sizes and terrorize anyone brave enough to go under the city.

    Possible Origin: There are many stories from the past 90 years of alligators found in streams, parks, bushes, even the rivers of New York, some of which were later found to be lizards. One "spinner of colorful yarns" actually claimed to have found a large number of alligators there but never proved any of his stories.

    Fact: Alligators cannot live in the cold temperatures of New York City, and they would die very quickly from the bacteria present in sewers. They have never been found there.

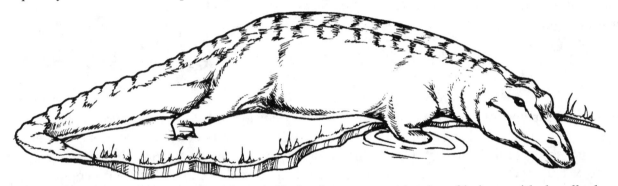

2. **Urban Myth:** Spiders will crawl into the hair of a person with a lot of hair or with dreadlocks and cause the person to grow sick and die.

    Possible Origin: People have often said that with some hairdos, a person might forego washing it in order to preserve the style.

    Fact: There is no known case of someone having died from a bite by a spider who set up residence in a person's hair.

3. **Urban Myth:** A woman dies of a heart attack after her husband calls her from his grave.

    Possible Origin: Some people's fear of being buried alive leads them to invent devices to put in a tomb so the dead can call out and say a mistake has been made.

    Fact: There have been no proven cases of the deceased giving the living a call on the telephone.

Activities

A. In groups of three or four, find and list several myths from *To Kill a Mockingbird*. These may be myths the children believe or ones believed by adults in the community. Record the myths, identify their sources, if you can find them, and tell what actually happened. Discuss the reasons you think the myths got started and why anyone would believe them.

B. Can you identify any such myths which have circulated around your school, your neighborhood, or your city? Report back to the class on what you have discovered.

The Great Depression

When the stock market crashed in 1929, America's economy had been deteriorating for several years. The government had a practice of not interfering with business practices in any way, and when the market crashed, the entire country went into a terrible period known as the Great Depression. During the first two years of the Depression these things happened:

- 25% of those wanting to work could not find jobs.

- The stock market lost 80% of its value in two years.

- Over 13 million people lost their jobs.

- Farm prices fell 53%.

- Thousands of banks closed because people panicked and withdrew their money.

- At least half of the American people lived below the subsistence level (that is, with less money than needed to pay for food and shelter).

Millions of people went hungry and lost their homes. Highways and cities became crowded with the homeless who often built Hoovervilles, communities where they scooped out underground hovels covered by sheets of tin in which to live. Once-wealthy businessmen jumped from high buildings to their deaths rather than to live with nothing. There was no Social Security to support people financially.

The physical troubles of the Depression also caused emotional depression in millions of people. The Depression lasted for years, never really ending until World War II began. Throughout these years, the poor were unbelievably destitute. Conditions for families like the Ewells were common. As sometimes happens when people are desperate, they begin to look for someone to blame (regardless of the truth), and this blame turns to hatred and fear. Consequently, one result of the misery in America during the Depression was the uprising of the Ku Klux Klan.

The Depression affected families in many different ways. People made do with less. Clothing was passed down from one child to another, and most were grateful to have someone else's hand-me-down clothing, shoes, and/or toys. What clothing that was new was usually made by hand, because few could afford to buy readymade clothing. Toys were handmade, also. Most people planted vegetable gardens and raised chickens for the eggs. Those who had no homes often ate in soup kitchens or worked for their meals, if they could find someone who had odd jobs to be done.

Activity

The attitudes and life habits of many people who lived through the Depression were changed, sometimes for the rest of their lives, even if they later made money and were no longer poor. Interview someone who lived through the Great Depression and was old enough at the time to remember it. This may be a great-grandparent or neighbor. Many of these people are now becoming quite old, and you may not know anyone who lived then. In that case, you might contact a nursing home or retirement center to find someone who lived at the time. This person may be able to come to your classroom to answer your questions. Follow the guidelines on the next page for your interview.

"The Great Depression" Interview Guidelines

When someone has given consent for you to interview him or her, it is important to remember that this person is doing you a favor. You must treat the person with respect and use good manners at all times. Ask your questions in a polite, considerate way. Remember to use the magic words of "please" and "thank you." Allow the person to finish answering one question before asking a new one. Smile. Be pleasant and kind. Remember that in the case of someone surviving today from the Great Depression, he or she has lived much longer than you, and you can learn a great deal from him or her. It may not seem so now, but someday, if you are fortunate and live a healthy life, you may be aged as well, so treat the person you are interviewing as you would like to be treated yourself.

Perhaps of most importance while conducting an interview is taking notes on the person's answers to your questions. Here are some questions you might ask:

- How old were you when you first knew about the Depression?

- How did the Depression affect your life?

- What was your family life like at the time?

- What did you do for entertainment then?

- Did your family have to move from one place to another during the Depression?

- What were some of the typical foods your family ate during the Depression years?

- What sorts of clothing did you wear, and where did you get it?

- Where did you live, and what was your home like?

- Did you ever know of hoboes or tramps who came around where you lived? What did they do?

- Did you listen to the radio during those years? Why, or why not?

- What kinds of toys did children play with back then?

- Did you grow any of your own food? If so, what kind?

- Did your family preserve food in any way? How?

- What kind of furniture did you have, and where did you get it?

- Did you know of any movie stars or musicians who were famous at the time? Who? Tell me about them and their work as well as your interest in them.

- How did life change for you after the Great Depression?

- Are there any lessons or fears you learned during the Depression that you keep with you today?

When your interview is finished, thank the person. Write a report about what you learned, and give a copy of your report to the person you interviewed as well as to your teacher.

Reading Response Journals

Good readers relate personally to what they read. They empathize with a story's characters and can imagine themselves in similar situations. They give meaning to a story even as they take meaning from it. Teaching your students new ways to relate to what they read can help them better understand and enjoy *To Kill a Mockingbird*.

- Reading response journals will enable students to enrich their experience of reading by giving it structure and form. In the journals, students are encouraged to respond in a variety of ways to their reading. Try some of these ideas with your students.

- Tell the students the purpose of the journals is to allow them to record their thoughts, observations, questions, and ideas as they read the book.

- Before students read a section or subsection, give them a specific question to consider while reading. Some sample questions may be found on page 39. Knowing these questions ahead of time allows students to focus on the ideas and insights you want them to get from their reading.

- Have students use the journals to take notes on cultural, historical, or social backgrounds which will help them better understand the novel's events.

- Record new vocabulary words in the journals, along with their definitions. This helps to keep the words and their meanings in the students' minds as they read, and it gives them a forum for using the words in their own sentences.

- Sometimes, instead of questions for them to answer in their journals, provide them with a sentence starter to complete as the beginning of a writing assignment. Always give the sentence starters which will make them think rather than just supply a missing word. Sample sentence starters can be found among the questions on page 39.

- Use a variety of reading strategies. Alternate oral reading with silent reading or allow students to follow along as you read to them. Accept questions and encourage them to comment about the content of the story. Point out literary terms and examples of literary techniques in the book and have students record them in their journals.

- Assure the students that although you may write comments and responses to their observations in their journals, the journals are private and will not be read in class or to others without the student's permission.

- Reserve a special time of each daily period for writing in the journals. Ten minutes is generally sufficient, but adapt the amount of time to your classroom situation.

- If possible, keep the journals in the classroom. This helps prevent them from being damaged on the school grounds and tells the students they are important for their learning.

- Make the journals a positive experience for the students. Some students will go on to keep private journals of their reading outside of class, and you will know you have given them yet another way to glean the most reading enjoyment they can.

Quiz Time!

1. List three important events from this section.

   _____

   _____

   _____

2. Why does Dill want to go for a walk, something no one in Maycomb ever does?

   _____

   _____

3. What strange thing becomes apparent when Jem goes to retrieve his pants?

   _____

   _____

4. How does Scout come to find a blanket around her shoulders after watching Miss Maudie's house burn?

   _____

   _____

5. Describe Tom Robinson and Atticus' relationship with him.

   _____

   _____

   _____

6. How does Atticus feel children's questions should be answered. Give an example.

   _____

   _____

   _____

7. Why does Atticus say, "It's a sin to kill a mockingbird," and what does he mean by it?

   _____

   _____

   _____

8. How does Calpurnia handle the situation when she sees the dog coming down the street?

   _____

   _____

9. Why does Atticus believe Mrs. DuBose has courage?

   _____

   _____

10. On the back of this page, tell about the local response to Atticus' decision to defend Tom Robinson. Include the incidents involving the children at school.

Who-I-Am Collages

This activity may be completed either in class or for homework. If it is to be completed in class, the students will need a bag or box in which to collect the items, pictures, and symbols they intend to use, and they will also need approximately one week to think about and plan for their collages. Assure students that this activity is not intended to invade their privacy in any way, nor is it to make them share something they feel uncomfortable sharing. They are only to use materials with which they are comfortable and to reveal only things about themselves they wish to reveal.

Have students follow these instructions.

1. Over the period of one week, students are to search through magazines, newspapers, photo albums, and their own rooms and lockers to collect newspaper clippings, advertisements, pictures, and small items which they feel say something about their own personalities. For example, someone who enjoys sports might save pictures or items having to do with the sports that student likes. Someone who enjoys music might save pieces of music, items about favorite recordings, or pictures of musicians they enjoy. They should save two kinds of items: ones which show aspects of themselves that others know and some which show aspects of themselves others do not know but which the individual would like them to know.

2. At the end of the week, the students are to arrange the items they have collected into collages. They can arrange the items in any way they wish and then bring their collages to class. It is a good idea for the teacher to make a collage of him or herself as well. Students enjoy seeing something about their teacher of which they had no previous knowledge, and the teacher's sharing assures the students that the teacher is willing to do what he or she asks the students to do. It helps establish trust between teacher and students.

3. When the collages have been assembled, discuss them as a class or in small, cooperative groups. The students will now begin to realize that just as each has previously kept some things hidden from their classmates, others have likewise done so, and they will begin to realize that their classmates are more complex than they may have thought. From this insight, it is a natural step to go on to a discussion about how everyone has aspects of him- or herself which are not always apparent to others. Students can also see the implications this has for relationships among people. They learn that one cannot always "tell a book by its cover" and that each of us has special qualities and abilities.

4. Discuss how most people tend to see only certain things about other people and how this can lead to stereotyping. For example, seeing only the color of a person's skin, the clothing he or she wears, or hearing the accent with which the person speaks without trying to see beneath the surface of that person can lead to faulty and unfair judgments. Discuss some possible ways in which they can recognize and correct this natural tendency in themselves in order to appreciate others more fully, as well as themselves.

Idioms

If you are reading something and cannot understand it, it may be that you do not understand the idioms. This is an especially common problem for a newcomer to a language. Idioms are phrases with meanings that do not fit exactly the definitions of the words in them. For examples, read the following paragraph.

Joe is a cool dude. He never loses it or gets mad, and he knows how to get his way. He is getting on in years and his face is a road map, but whenever he tuckers out, he takes it easy until he is back in shape. He takes care of himself, and handling things is a breeze for him.

Although you would not turn in this paragraph as part of an essay, many speakers of English talk like this when they are speaking to each other. Here is a more formal way of writing the paragraph.

Joe is a calm person. He never loses control of his emotions or becomes angry, and he knows how to get what he wants. He is getting old and his face is wrinkled, but when he gets tired, he rests until he feels well again. He follows good health practices, and he is easily able to do what he needs to do.

To Kill a Mockingbird contains many idioms. Here are some of them.

- made a pile
- related by blood
- bound and determined
- took his time
- money changed hands
- honest day's work
- get someone's goat

- had it coming to him
- reduce to dust
- mind his own business
- pitch dark
- you mind your mother
- keep in fits
- acid tongue

- born and bred
- bought cotton
- wear us out
- tell on someone
- give up
- in a blaze of glory
- high and mighty

With some of these, you can nearly tell what they mean by the words in them. With others, it is not so easy.

Activities

1. In groups of four or five, decide what you think each of the above idioms mean. Come back together as a class and share your opinions. What do they really mean?

2. Again, in groups of four or five, divide this section of the book into segments. Each person should take one segment and read through it. List any idioms you find.

3. Find more about idioms at this Internet site, the ESL idiom page: *http://www.pacificnet.net/ ~sperling/idioms.cgi*

The Scourge of Rabies

When Calpurnia sees the dog walking lopsided down the street, she immediately knows what is wrong with him—he has rabies. Rabies is a terrible disease, but it seldom affects domestic animals today. Most pets are vaccinated for the disease when young, but during the 1930s when people could not afford to pay for shots for their pets, it was still a common occurrence.

Rabies is caused by a virus which is passed from one animal to another through a bite that breaks the skin. All warm-blooded animals can get rabies, including dogs and humans. It is almost always fatal unless a painful series of vaccine injections is given to the person bitten. Most cases of rabies today are due to the bite of a wild animal like a skunk, raccoon, or bat.

Here is what happens when a person gets rabies. There is an incubation period of several weeks, and then the person becomes depressed, anxious, and irritable and begins to have trouble breathing and swallowing. He becomes extremely thirsty but cannot drink. Thick mucous collects in his throat, and in terror, he vomits. A fever rises while the person has seizures, paralysis, and eventually enters a coma. This lasts for three to five days until the person dies from the encephalitis which the virus causes and during which the virus reproduces, moving along nerves to the brain.

Two forms of rabies affect animals: furious rabies and dumb rabies. Furious rabies follows the same course as rabies in humans, and the animal, which becomes very irritable and bites and snaps at any living thing it encounters. In dumb rabies, there is little or no irritable stage, and the animal becomes paralyzed before it dies.

The way in which rabies is spread was first recognized in 1804, and in 1884 Louis Pasteur developed a successful vaccine. Today an anti-rabies serum is injected in the person who has been bitten by a rabid animal, and this is followed by a fourteen to thirty-day course of daily, painful, vaccine injections. Booster shots are given ten and twenty days later. Human rabies immune globulin is also given.

Activity

Until this century, many infectious diseases abounded. Antibiotics to cure the infections had not yet been discovered, nor had inoculations been developed to prevent people from catching them. At any time, a family might be decimated or wiped out by some terrible, contagious disease. Now we have vaccinations for many of these diseases and antibiotics to treat them.

Research one of the following diseases which has plagued humans. Write a paper describing the disease, its cause, its treatment, and whether or not it has been eradicated.

• poliomyelitis	• scarlet fever
• tuberculosis	• measles
• mumps	• chicken pox
• cholera	• bubonic plague
• hantavirus	• Aquired Immuno-deficiency Syndrome (AIDS virus)
• smallpox	• Ebola virus

Report back to your class on what you learn. Present your findings to your class as an oral report. With your presentation include a visual aid such as a poster, chart, or illustration of the disease's symptoms.

Role-Play

Sometimes it helps students to recognize more easily what is really happening in a situation when they are able to put themselves physically into a scene. Ask for students to volunteer for this activity. Do not require it of anyone because some students may be uncomfortable participating in such an activity. Even so, the students who do not participate can benefit by watching and listening to others do it.

Call two student volunteers to the front of the classroom. Tell them one should pretend to be a twelve-year-old brother and the other to be his eight-year-old sister. They will act as these people in one of the following situations.

- One night the older brother and his friend are going to spy on a neighbor who they think is a little strange. Their parents have gone to dinner. Since the brother is supposed to be in charge of the sister, he wants her to go with him and his friend, but she is afraid to do so. He does not want to leave her in the house alone, and she does not want to go with him.

- The brother and sister are walking home from school one day, and they see two sticks of chewing gum on the fencepost of the house where the "strange" neighbor lives. The next day they find a watch, and the following day they find some shiny dimes.

- The sister, who is a tomboy and likes to fight, is angry. A boy at school has called her father a bad name, and she does not like it one bit. The brother tries to calm her down, but she is determined to let the name-caller have it.

- The sister gets the BB gun she wanted for Christmas, and she is pointing it at a neighbor whom she does not like. She does not intend to shoot the neighbor and is just pretending; however, the brother does not think she should even be pretending to do such a thing.

- Standing on the porch one day the brother and sister notice a dog coming down the street. They recognize the dog as belonging to a neighbor, but the dog is acting strangely and walking funny with drool coming from his mouth.

- The children are caught playing a trick on a cranky old lady who lives down the street. Their punishment is to read to the old lady for an hour every day for over two weeks. They feel their punishment is unjust and want their father to change his mind about it.

- The brother wants to go to the video arcade with his friends, and his little sister wants to go with them.

After completing each role-play, discuss as a class what occurred. Would everyone have done the same things? Why or why not?

Quiz Time!

1. List three important events from this section.

   _____

   _____

   _____

2. How does Calpurnia make the children dress when she takes them to church?

   _____

   _____

3. How does Calpurnia's son learn to read? _____

   _____

4. With what is Aunt Alexandria most preoccupied?

   _____

   _____

5. Tell the story about who is under Scout's bed, and explain how and why that person is there.

   _____

   _____

6. What does Mr. Sam Levy tell the Ku Klux Klan when they parade past his house?

   _____

   _____

7. Why does Atticus sit outside the jail, and what happens?

   _____

   _____

   _____

8. To what does Atticus compare the men who come to the jail and why?

   _____

   _____

   _____

9. Where do the children go to watch Tom Robinson's trial and with whom?

   _____

   _____

10. On the back of this page, respond to the following: Aunt Alexandria first tries to get Atticus to fire Calpurnia, and then she tries to get him to stop the children from speaking about certain things when she is in the house. Describe at least one of these scenes. Why do you think Atticus insists on Calpurnia's staying to help raise the children?

Southern Cooking

Certain foods have come to be synonymous with the southeastern part of the United States, such as Southern fried chicken, fried catfish, hush puppies, fried okra, potato salad, and sweet tea. The mere mention of these foods is enough to water the mouth of a southerner who has moved to another part of the country or world. Below are three recipes for southern foods.

Green Pea Salad

Ingredients:

- 3 cups (720 mL) cooked fresh or frozen garden peas
- 3 chopped hard-boiled eggs
- ½ cup (120 mL) chopped onion
- salt and pepper to taste
- mayonnaise to moisten mixture
- lettuce

Preparation: Mix ingredients together to the consistency of potato salad. Chill and serve on lettuce leaves.

Hush Puppies

Ingredients:

- 2 cups (480 mL) cornmeal
- 1 tablespoon (15 mL) flour
- ½ teaspoon (2.5 mL) soda
- 1 teaspoon (5 mL) baking powder
- cooking oil
- 1 teaspoon (5 mL) salt
- 3–6 tablespoons (45–90 mL) chopped onion (according to taste)
- 1 cup (240 mL) buttermilk
- 1 egg, beaten

Preparation: Combine the dry ingredients and add the onion. Add the milk and then the egg. Drop the mixture by spoonfuls into a deep fryer filled with oil and fry to a golden brown. The hush puppies will float to the top when done if they are fried in a deep kettle. (**Safety Note:** Be very careful when cooking with hot oil, and do this activity only under the supervision of an adult. Use protection on your hands and body, and never drop or splash water or liquid into hot oil.)

Banana Pudding with Vanilla Wafers

Ingredients:

- 1 package of vanilla or banana pudding (the kind you cook)
- 2 cups (480 mL) milk
- 3 fresh bananas
- half a small package of vanilla wafers
- whipped cream or prepared whipped topping

Preparation: Prepare pudding with milk according to the directions on the box. Slice the bananas into slices about ¼ inch (.6 cm) thick. Line the bottom of a 1.5 quart (1.5 L) bowl with vanilla wafers. Cover the wafers with one layer of sliced bananas. Pour one-third of the pudding on top of the wafers. Continue layering pudding, bananas, and wafers until all are used. Serve topped with whipped cream or whipped topping.

Growing Up a Lady

Aunt Alexandria and Jem just cannot understand why Scout will not act more like a young lady. "Acting like a lady" was considered to be a very important goal for white girls growing up in the 1930s. This piece printed by J.B. Lippincott in 1920 tells just what was meant by that.

We must persistently strive against selfishness, ill-temper, irritability, indolence. It is impossible for the self-centered or ill-tempered girl to win love and friends.

One of the greatest blemishes in the character of any young person, especially of any young girl or woman, is forwardness, boldness, pertness. The young girl who acts in such a manner as to attract attention in public; who speaks loudly, and jokes and laughs and tells stories in order to be heard by others than her immediate companions, . . . who expresses opinions on all subjects with forward self-confidence, is rightly regarded by all thoughtful and cultivated people as one of the most disagreeable and obnoxious characters to meet with in society.

Women of "good families" who grew up in the South during this time had to meet further expectations. They were expected to be church members, to speak softly and with a certain accent unlike those of their poor neighbors. Integrity was very important. One could never steal, cheat, or speak badly to someone who could not speak back, such as someone of a lower class or a non-white. They were expected to help take care of their less fortunate neighbors while allowing their own children to be cared for by black nurses who taught them to be honest and "Christian."

Girl children played with non-white children and had them to their houses, but they never went to the houses of non-white friends. They played jumprope and jacks and skated. They almost always wore dresses, and they never wore slacks or jeans to school. Girls were expected always to be neat and clean with their hair curled.

Little girls dressed up in the afternoons to look like Shirley Temple, a famous movie star who was always dressed perfectly with every hair in place. They never went barefoot or fought. Their speech was expected to be grammatical at all times, and they could never curse or swear. They never said things like "shut up," and they did not play cards or go to movies on Sunday. Theirs was a very circumscribed world.

Activity

In groups of four or five, make three lists: one list of the ways girls and women were expected to behave in the 1930s, one list of the ways they are expected to act today, and one list showing how girls were free to act in both times.

Use the lists you have made as the basis for a compare-and-contrast essay. Directions for how to write a five-paragraph essay are on page 37. You may also find instructions on how to write this kind of essay at the following Internet sites.

LEO Comparison/Contrast Essays: *http://leo.stcloud.msus.edu/acadwrite/comparcontrast.html*

Guide to Grammar and Writing: *http://webster.commnet.edu/HP/pages/darling/grammar.htm*

Similes and Metaphors

Similes and metaphors are comparisons between two things to create images in the reader's mind. Similes compare two things with the use of the words "like" or "as." "Standing stiff as a stork" is a simile that compares someone standing still just as a stork does, and one can imagine a stork, one leg up behind it. Metaphors compare two things as though they were the same thing. "Summer was Dill" is a metaphor that says summer and Scout's friend, Dill, were the same to her because Scout always associated summer with their adventures together at that time.

Some of the similes Harper Lee uses in this section of the book include the following. The key words are in bold print to help you recognize what makes each phrase a simile.

- Ladies were **like** soft teacakes with frosting of sweat and sweet talcum.
- The Radley place . . . drew Dill **as** the moon draws water.
- Jem waved my words away **as** if fanning gnats.
- Smoke was rolling off our house . . . **like** fog off a riverbank.
- . . . suspend in a thin layer of ice **like** a fly in amber.
- He shivered **like** a rabbit.
- . . . screaming **like** a stuck hog.

Some of the metaphors in the book include these. The words in parentheses name the two things being compared.

- I never loved to read. One does not love breathing. (*reading* and *breathing*)
- . . . tinfoil . . . winking at me in the afternoon sun. (*tinfoil* and *something with eyes*)
- Jem's mind was racing. (*mind* and *something which moves quickly*)
- He began pouring out our secrets right and left. (*secrets* and *something pourable*)
- I should be a ray of sunshine in my father's lonely life. (*Scout* and *a bright ray of light*)
- Time had slowed to a nauseating crawl. (*time* and *something which crawls*)
- . . . walls of a pink penitentiary closing in on me. (*walls* and *something that moves*)
- Shadows became substance. (*shadows* and *something you can feel*)

Activities

1. Find three more similes in this section of the book and write them on the back of this paper.
2. Find three more metaphors in this section of the book and write them on the back of this paper.
3. Write a simile and a metaphor of your own.
4. Write a paragraph describing one of the following, using at least one simile and one metaphor.
   - a scene at the beach or the lake
   - an auto race
   - a fashion show
   - Saturday afternoon at the shopping mall
   - a school assembly

Allusions

When Calpurnia tells Jem and Scout she is going to take them to church with her, Scout recalls a not-very-nice trick her Sunday school class once played on Eunice Ann Simpson. They tied her to a chair in the furnace room and then went off and forgot her until Eunice managed to make a ruckus, disrupting the service upstairs and saying she didn't want to "play Shadrach any more." This expression, "play Shadrach," is an allusion to a story in the Bible's Old Testament in which three Hebrew children named Shadrach, Meshach, and Abednego are thrown into a fiery furnace by the king and are later found unharmed.

Allusions are references made to something or someone in another time or place or in another piece of writing. An author frequently uses allusions to relate something else to what is presently happening in a story. It is a form of imagery like similes, metaphors, and personification.

Common things to which a writer might allude are Biblical stories, stories from mythology, legends, and history. Sometimes titles of books are themselves allusions, such as John Steinbeck's *East of Eden* (from the Bible) and Ernest Hemingway's *For Whom the Bell Tolls* (from a poem by John Donne).

Activity

The following is a list of allusions. Name the famous person(s) or place(s), fictional or real, to which these phrases refer.

1. "To be or not to be, that is the question." _____

2. Bloody Mary _____

3. The Third Reich _____

4. *Il Duce* _____

5. Good Queen Bess _____

6. The Genius of Menlo Park _____

7. "I Have a Dream" _____

8. "We have nothing to fear but fear itself." _____

9. David and his harp _____

10. Garden of Eden _____

11. *der Führer* _____

12. star-crossed lovers _____

Quiz Time!

1. List three important events from this section of the book.

   _____

   _____

   _____

2. What does Mayella think of Atticus? _____

   _____

   _____

3. How does Mayella respond when Atticus asks her if she loves her father?

   _____

   _____

4. Why does Atticus think Tom Robinson could not have beaten Mayella as she says he did?

   _____

   _____

5. What big mistake does Tom Robinson make during his testimony?

   _____

   _____

6. How do the children learn that Mr. Dolphus Raymond is not what they think he is?

   _____

   _____

7. When and how does Atticus learn the children were in the courtroom?

   _____

   _____

8. What is Jem's reaction to the jury's verdict? _____

   _____

   _____

9. What does Atticus do when Robert Ewell spits in his face and threatens to kill him?

   _____

   _____

10. On the back of this page, write your response to the following: After Tom Robinson is convicted of beating and raping Mayella Ewell, the Negro people in the balcony all stand to honor Atticus as he is walking out of the courtroom door. This is a very powerful scene. Why do they show him in this way that they consider him a hero?

Characterization Chart

A writer uses four main ways to tell about characters: what they say, how they look (including mannerisms, habits, etc.), what they do, and what others say about them. Have the students complete this characterization chart individually or in small groups for the main characters in *To Kill a Mockingbird*. Then as a class, transfer the information to a large poster to display on the classroom wall. Refer to the chart and change it as the class reads the book. Consider as a class: Do first impressions stay the same throughout the book?

	Scout	Jem	Atticus	Dill
Self Descriptions				
Typical Sayings				
Appearances				
Favorite Pastimes				
Important Actions				
Treatment of Others				
Beliefs				
What Others Think/Say				

Setting

Along with characters and plot, setting is one of the three main elements of a story. Setting is the place and time of a story, but it is also more. In a different setting, the characters would be different people with different personalities, beliefs, and lifestyles. Scout would not be the same Scout we see in *To Kill a Mockingbird* if she were born and raised in New York City, or San Francisco, or Salt Lake City. The town and house where she is growing up in Maycomb, Alabama, have shaped and formed her into the person she is just as much as Atticus and Calpurnia have.

How is this true? Several things in a setting contribute to how a story and characters take form, including weather, location, economy, and history.

Weather determines what kinds of plants grow and how people spend their winters and summers, their days and nights. People are likely to have a different attitude about a climate with frequent, heavy rainfalls than they do concerning one with long, hot, dry summers and cold, bleak winters. They wear different clothing, eat different foods, and spend their leisure time doing different things.

Life in a small town in Alabama in the 1930s was very different from life in a large eastern city of the present day. Streets were narrow and often made of dirt where children played ball and an occasional car chugged by; today, wide boulevards are filled with blaring taxis and lined with shops. In the small town of the book, neighbors knew each other's deep, dark secrets. They were not strangers living side by side, one in millions of city dwellers.

People in a rural, small-town economy think differently about what material goods are important. In 1930s Maycomb, most people cared most about having enough to eat and a protective home. Much of what they ate they grew themselves or traded with others. They had no need for supermarkets or shopping malls. In fact, none existed. They also shared a history. Unlike a large city where people come together from somewhere else with different backgrounds, languages, and ideas about what is important in life, the people of Maycomb shared most of those things in common.

Activity

In groups of four or five, develop the setting for a story based on where you live. Do the following:

- Describe how your setting looks, including the homes, schools, and roads.

- Describe the most common lifestyles of the people.

- Describe how people make money and how that affects the way they live. Do they raise their own food? shop in huge shopping areas? drive cars or ride mass transit?

- Describe the history of the people. Do they share a common one, or do they come from many different backgrounds and speak different languages?

When it is complete, share your writing with the class. Do all your classmates live in the same setting as you do? What is alike? What is different? Discuss this as a class.

Character Analysis

An activity you will frequently be asked to do in literature classes is write a character analysis, which means you must look carefully at a character and describe the character in detail. You must tell what kind of person the character is, what he/she does and says, and why you think he/she does and says these things. The three items you need to look at most closely are the character's motivations, values, and reactions to situations.

First list your answers to these questions when analyzing a character:

- What does the character do most of the time, and how does he/she do it?

- Does the character say what he/she really means, or does he/she mean something other than what he/she says?

- Why does the character do what he/she does?

- On what does the character place high value in terms of money, fame, material possessions, family, and so forth?

- Does the character have a high standard of ethics? Is he/she honest, compassionate, and responsible? Does he/she have integrity?

- Is the character consistent? Does he/she behave similarly in all situations?

- Identify a situation which shows the true personality of the character. How does he/she react under pressure? Is he/she logical and reasonable?

Activity

You will complete a character analysis. Follow these steps.

1. Choose a character in *To Kill a Mockingbird* to analyze.

2. Compile a list of the character traits your character exhibits in the novel.

3. Write a five-paragraph essay in which you analyze the character, following the structure described below or the directions given on page 37.

   - Write a first paragraph which introduces the character about whom you are writing and the main idea of what you wish to say about that character. This paragraph should contain your thesis statement.

   - Write three paragraphs which go into detail about your character. Use evidence from the novel and from the list you have compiled. Concentrate each paragraph on a character trait you have identified, and show why that trait is present.

   - Write a final paragraph in which you "wrap up" your essay and show why your thesis statement has been proven by the evidence presented.

Adult Conversations

Scout is a child throughout *To Kill a Mockingbird*. She is eight years old when she watches from the balcony while Atticus cross-examines Robert Ewell. Mr. Ewell tells a descriptive and ugly story about Tom Robinson attacking his daughter, Mayella. It is all lies, but he tells it for everyone to hear.

Many people (probably including Atticus himself, had he known the children were watching the trial) would agree that a child of eight should not be exposed to what was happening in that courtroom. The scenes are graphic. Robert Ewell does not seem to care who hears what he has to say, and he wants to make his story as colorful and descriptive as he can in much the same way he might tell a story to his cronies in a saloon or behind the fence somewhere. Of course, he is supposed to answer with the truth as he has sworn to do, but this does not keep him from lying.

Once the testimony begins, Scout has absolutely no intention of leaving the courtroom. She is glued to her seat. By and large, Atticus has treated her as an adult most of her life, allowing her to hear what adults in her house have to say about anything and anyone and allowing her to speak her own mind at all times, even when Aunt Alexandria or Miss Caroline believe he should protect her from what some would consider adult topics. She has been following the progress of the trial avidly, and even though she does not know all that the adults are saying, she is a very bright child and understands most of it.

When Rev. Sykes suddenly realizes the content of what Robert Ewell has to say about Tom Robinson, he tries to have Jem take Scout from the courtroom, not wanting her to hear anything inappropriate. One could argue that if Rev. Sykes really believed this to be true, he should not have allowed the children to go into the courthouse balcony in the first place. After all, he knew this was going to be a rape trial, so what did he expect? However, the description given by Mr. Ewell is uglier than Rev. Sykes anticipated, and he wants Scout protected.

But Scout has no intention of leaving her place in the courtroom. She wants to see the trial to the end. After all, she has watched everything to this point. Trying to get her out of there now would be a little like trying to stop a flood once the dam has broken.

Activity

Should children be allowed to hear anything and everything? On the back of this paper write one page, beginning with one of these statements:

- Children should be allowed to listen in on adult conversations, whatever their topics, because . . .

- Children should be protected from adult conversations about things they are too young to understand because . . .

Quiz Time!

1. List three important events from this section.

   _____

   _____

   _____

2. Why do the adults in Maycomb never talk about the Tom Robinson case?

   _____

   _____

   _____

3. What does Mr. Link Deas do when he learns that Helen Robinson is walking a mile out of her way to go to work each day?

   _____

   _____

   _____

4. What character does Scout play in the school pageant?

   _____

5. On what does Scout "squander" her thirty cents? _____

6. Why can't Scout change back into her clothes on the way home?

   _____

   _____

7. Describe the scene in the woods on the way home from the school pageant.

   _____

   _____

   _____

8. Who does Mr. Heck Tate find under a tree, and what is wrong with him?

   _____

   _____

9. How does Scout learn who her protector had been?

   _____

   _____

10. On the back of this page, write what you think is the meaning of this sentence. "Atticus had used every tool available to free men to save Tom Robinson, but in the secret courts of men's hearts Atticus had no case."

Bookworm

Scout is a bookworm. She once says, "I did not love reading. One does not love breathing," meaning that books are as important to her as her very life. They keep her alive just as food and water do, because they are something she needs.

A bookworm is literally an insect which feeds on books, so a person who loves books, who "feeds" on them mentally and emotionally, is often called a bookworm. The name aptly fits Scout.

There is a way to make a book report which looks like a giant bookworm. As you read *To Kill a Mockingbird*, make note of its themes, characters, setting, plot, idioms, similes, metaphors, and allusions to complete your own bookworm report. Follow these directions.

Materials:

- seven 6" (15 cm) round pieces of construction paper or tagboard
- one 5" (12.5 cm) round piece of construction paper or tagboard
- 1 chenille stick
- 7 brass paper fasteners
- 2 or 3 pieces of wire or fishing line of suitable length for hanging

Directions:

1. On the smaller round of construction paper, draw a mouth and eyes to make a face. Also write the title and author of the novel.

2. Cut the chenille stick in half. Attach the pieces to either side at the top of the circle for feelers.

3. On each of the seven larger rounds, in your best handwriting, write a paragraph on the following:

   - themes
   - characters
   - setting
   - plot
   - idioms
   - similes and metaphors
   - allusions

3. Attach the circles together in a row with paper fasteners with the face at the head and with the writing all facing downward.

4. Hang the bookworm from the ceiling by wire or fishing line. When a breeze wafts through the room or someone walks by, the bookworm will dance in the breeze.

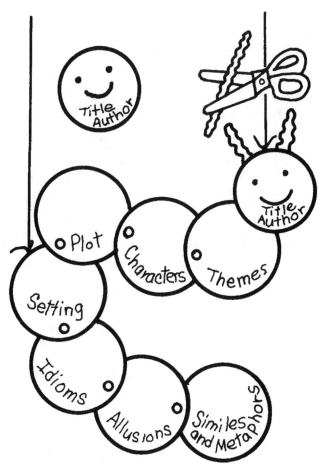

Themes

The theme of a story is the story's main idea. The theme of a fable is its moral. The theme of a parable would be the lesson it teaches. The theme of a novel is what it tells us about life and the ways people behave. You are not told directly in the novel, "This is the theme of this book," or "This is what I, the author, want you to understand when you read my book." You must figure out for yourself what the theme is by looking at the characters, what they do and say, and what happens in the book. The theme is the truth the author wishes to show. Most books have more than one theme.

In *To Kill a Mockingbird,* there are many themes upon which you could base a paper. There is the theme of stereotypes in which the nature of stereotypes is explored, whether racial, social, or gender based. There is the theme of what a hero is and how courage works in the lives of Atticus, Scout, and Tom Robinson. There is the theme of family. What is a family? How do single parents raise children? How are children initiated into the adult world? There is the theme of how children can sometimes form a bridge between social classes and races or between perceived insiders and outsiders. There is the theme of violence and different ways of dealing with it.

To Kill a Mockingbird is also a novel about the growth and development of a child. In the book, Scout, Jem, and Dill grow from one stage of life into a new and more adult stage by being confronted with some harsh realities of their world. They see things that are hard to witness, but by doing so they mature and gain better judgment. The novel is a "rite of passage" book, or *bildungsroman* (German, for "a novel of development").

Activity

In groups of three or four, brainstorm the themes you see in this novel, and list them. Which themes do you think are most important? Why? Examine them carefully.

If you think there are stereotypes, why? What is a stereotype? How do stereotypes begin, and how do they grow? Why do people sometimes seem to need stereotypes? What is the danger in them? Identify a character in *To Kill a Mockingbird* who is a portrayed stereotypically, and explain how you can tell a character who is stereotypical and one who is not.

If you think the treatment of families is the novel's most important theme, discuss why you believe this. What is a family? Does a family consist of a mother, a father, and two children? Or can a family be more or less than that? How many kinds of families do you know? Is a family only those people who live in a house together? Or can a family be larger, more extended?

After you have brainstormed your ideas and chosen a theme you feel to be the most important, write on your own a five-paragraph essay on that theme. Information about writing a five-paragraph essay can be found on page 37.

Racial Hatred and Discrimination

During the time Scout and Jem were growing up in Maycomb, a terrible new day was dawning across the Atlantic Ocean in Germany. Adolf Hitler, furious that Germany had lost World War I and resentful of the extreme punishments which had been directed against Germany for having begun the war, decided he wanted to be a political leader who would lead Germany to a great new future.

Hitler based his ideas about this wonderful new world on racial hatred, especially his hatred of Jews. Germany was in a Great Depression even worse than the one in the United States, and many people were starving. The reparations the other countries of Europe had demanded of Germany left many Germans very angry, and in their desperation, they followed Hitler's lead. Before he was finished, millions of innocent people had been killed, and much of Europe was destroyed.

After the South was defeated in the American Civil War, many people were uprooted from their homes and many were killed. The so-called Reconstruction Period following the war made things even worse. Only the wealthy could afford education, and just as in Germany, masses of people were angry and desperate. Not all Southerners hated the former slaves, but many blamed them for their troubles.

When people are desperate, they often look for someone to blame for their misfortunes. In Germany, they blamed the Jews. In the United States, the blacks were blamed. People thought that if it had not been for them, there would have been no war. If a person wants to look down on someone, that person will usually find someone worse off than him or herself. It helps if that person is someone who cannot fight back. Many groups arose to make sure the blacks "stayed in their place," including the Ku Klux Klan, a group of hate-filled men who made it their purpose not to allow black people to get jobs or have the same rights they claimed for themselves.

Activities

Complete one of the following.

1. Nearly everyone has experienced some form of prejudice or discrimination at some point in his or her life or has been treated unfairly for "being different." This may have been for looking different in some way. It may have been for not being good at sports or for having a physical disability. It may have been for being a girl. Write an essay about such a situation in your own life, how you handled it, and how it made you feel.

2. Draw a map of Europe to show the growth of Nazism there. Show which countries were overtaken by Hitler and when, what the Jewish and "non-Aryan" population of those countries was at the time, and how many people within that group were killed or deported to concentration camps by the Nazis.

3. Research a racially based supremacist group in the United States. When and how was it formed? What sorts of people belong to it and how many? What are their beliefs? Why do they believe they are better than the people they hate? Share what you learn with the class.

Boo's Diary

The plot of a story consists of the events in it. One event follows another, which in turn is followed by another, until a high point in the intensity of the story occurs and the story draws to a conclusion. Most novels have more than one plot. Two plots run alongside each other in *To Kill a Mockingbird*.

The main plot is about Tom Robinson, who is accused of beating and raping Mayella Ewell. Tom is accused, Atticus is named defense attorney, the children are threatened, and Atticus is called names because he truly tries to give Tom the best defense possible. Some men attempt to take Tom from the jail, Scout shames them out of it, they go to court, and so on. The climax comes when Tom is shot. In this plot, Scout watches what happens and tells the story.

The secondary plot is about the children's fascination with the mysterious and reclusive Boo. They imagine all sorts of things about him: what he might have done, what he will do. Then they have mysterious encounters with him, which they do not recognize at first as having to do with him. Scout also tells us this part of the story, but much of what happens, or might have happened, is in Scout's imagination. We never see the story from Boo's point of view, the way he sees it.

For all we know, Boo never speaks. We hear what the children imagine and fantasize about him and we hear what people like Atticus, Calpurnia, and Miss Maudie have to say about him, but Boo himself never speaks. All we know for sure about Boo are the few little glimpses of what Scout actually sees him do and what Jem, Dill, and Scout learn he has done. We do not know his feelings toward any of the events of the novel except for what we can glean from his actions.

Activity

In this activity you will have to use your imagination. Although Boo does not speak, we do know that he understands at least part of what other people say and do. He carries out his actions silently. He leaves objects. He helps. But he does not speak.

You are going to write a diary for Boo, but since Boo does not speak, you cannot write it in words.

Using drawings, pictographs you invent, pictures you cut from magazines, and/or small objects, "write" a diary for Boo. What do you think he is thinking as he goes through the events of the story and his part of the plot? How does he see those events? How does he see the children? What does he think is happening? How can you show what he thinks is happening without words?

When you finish your silent diary, share it with the class and answer questions about it.

The Five-Paragraph Essay

Learning to write a five-paragraph essay is one of the most useful things you can do. You will write these essays all through junior high school, high school, and college, and you can use the same principles of writing throughout your life, especially as part of an occupation or profession in which you are required to write reports of various kinds. Master this basic format now, and writing will be that much easier for you in the future. Here is the basic format:

- The first paragraph introduces the main idea of what you wish to say. This paragraph will contain your thesis statement.

- The next three paragraphs go into detail about your main idea and illustrate or prove it.

- The final paragraph "wraps up" your essay, stating why your thesis has been proven or illustrated through the evidence presented.

The first paragraph is your **introduction**. You capture your reader's attention in this paragraph. You must always write for your reader, whether the reader is your teacher, your employer, or any other audience. This first paragraph grabs the reader's interest in your topic, gives background on it, and leads your reader to the main idea you want him or her to take from your paper. You may write it before or after you write the main body of your essay. You may write a rough introduction first and then revise it after the rest of your essay is finished. When you write it is not the important thing; that you do write it is. There is no set number of sentences you must write in your introduction, although most introductions will have from four to eight sentences, and the last sentence will lead into your second paragraph.

The **body of your essay** consists of three paragraphs. Each paragraph will contain a main idea supporting what you have written in your thesis statement in the first paragraph, and each paragraph will have a separate main idea. In these paragraphs you provide the details that lead you to form your thesis. The last sentence of each paragraph will end with a sentence which brings the main idea of the paragraph to a close and leads into the next paragraph.

The **conclusion of your essay** is in the final paragraph. Its purpose is to wrap up the main idea, or thesis, of the essay. This paragraph will not introduce any new ideas. Instead, you will restate your thesis and summarize what you have written, but in different words. It is the most important paragraph of your essay, because it is the one your reader will most remember. Your conclusion will emphasize the significance of the thesis statement, complete the essay, and leave a final impression on your reader.

Activity

Choose a theme from *To Kill a Mockingbird* and following the above steps, write a five-paragraph essay about that theme with an introduction, a body, and a conclusion.

Symbols in *To Kill a Mockingbird*

Several things are symbolic in *To Kill a Mockingbird*. The most obvious symbol is the mockingbird itself. Scout asks Miss Maudie why Atticus told her it is a sin to kill a mockingbird. She has never known of her father to call anything a sin before. Miss Maudie tells her it is because a mockingbird never hurts anything and spends its whole life giving pleasure with its singing. It is wrong to kill something which does that.

This concept is important in several ways. It provides the title of the book, and the mockingbird symbolizes certain people in the book who give pleasure and do good for others. The primary person symbolized by the mockingbird is Tom Robinson. After he helps a poor, ignorant girl, she turns on him and, with her father, causes his death. In a symbolic sense, the Ewells and the jury who find Tom guilty kill the mockingbird.

The mockingbird also symbolizes Boo Radley who, in his own quiet, reclusive way, gives pleasure to the children by leaving small surprises for them. Boo is not killed; however, society is cruel to him, which Atticus considers almost as bad.

Finally, the mockingbird symbolizes Scout. As narrator of the story she "sings a song," and she is almost killed by the same person who caused Tom Robinson's death. Both Boo and Tom Robinson are at the mercy of the society in which they live, just as a wild bird is at the mercy of hunters and a child is at the mercy of adults.

Most good pieces of literature have such symbols to enhance the story's meaning. Birds are among the list of common symbols in stories and poems; others include colors, flowers, trees, snakes, and more.

Activity

Answer or respond to the following.

1. How do these serve as symbols in *To Kill a Mockingbird*?

     the mad dog: _____

     the tree house: _____

     the gun: _____

     the jury: _____

2. If you have ever heard a mockingbird sing, you will probably never forget its song. Research the mockingbird. Write a paragraph on the back of this paper, telling about it and its many voices.

3. How would you feel if you found a mockingbird which had been shot by a hunter?

     _____

     _____

     _____

     _____

     _____

Sample Journal Questions and Sentence Starters

Section 1 (Chapters 1–5)

- What does Scout mean when she says Mr. Radley "bought cotton"?
- Why does Miss Caroline not want Scout's father to teach her to read?
- Describe Walter Cunningham and his family.
- How does Dill arrive from Meridian his second summer in Maycomb?
- My idea of a hero is _____ because . . .
- Scout and Jem are intrigued by Dill because . . .
- Miss Caroline is insensitive to her students' needs by . . .
- Dill likes to play the villain in the children's make-believe plays, and when he does, he . . .

Section 2 (Chapters 6–11)

- Why do the children want to peek into the Radley's window?
- How does Jem walk when he gets into the sixth grade and why?
- Why does Atticus tell Jem and Scout they have to change their snowman?
- How and why does Miss Maudie's house look like a pumpkin?
- Jem gets off the fence by . . .
- Jem wants Scout to act . . .
- When Maycomb gets its first snowfall, Jem and Scout . . .
- Aunt Alexandria wants Scout to . . .

Section 3 (Chapters 12–17)

- Why do the men take off their hats and the women act respectfully when Jem and Scout walk into the black church with Calpurnia?
- What kind of folks are the Ewells?
- Why does Scout think she is being put into a "pink penitentiary?"
- Describe the night Atticus goes to the Maycomb County Jail and what happens.
- Jem thinks the black people in the church do not want him and Scout there because . . .
- Aunt Alexandria is the kind of person who . . .
- When Jem swipes the broom under Scout's bed, . . .
- Dill prefers a world of . . .

Section 4 (Chapters 18–25)

- Why is Mayella afraid of Atticus in the courtroom?
- Who is Mr. Dolphus Raymond?
- Describe Mr. Gilmer's attitude toward Tom in the courtroom.
- What do the black people of Maycomb send Atticus and why?
- Mayella says when Tom attacked her, she . . .
- Tom says when he walked by the Ewell house on his way to work, . . .
- Tom had been given thirty days in jail once for . . .
- When Calpurnia finds the children in the courtroom, she . . .

Section 5 (Chapters 26–31)

- Why does Helen Robinson fall down when Atticus drives up to her house?
- How does Atticus react when Scout mentions still wanting to see Boo?
- What is Jem trying hard to forget and why?
- Where are the Ewell children when Mr. Link Deas stops by with Helen and why?
- Mr. Underhill, writing in the newspaper, likens Tom's death to . . .
- The burden of giving current events reports falls to the town children because . . .
- The scratching Judge Taylor hears at his screen one night is probably . . .
- The Halloween after Tom Robinson was killed changed from how it was celebrated before by . . .

Any Questions?

When you finished reading the book, did you have any questions? Were there things left unanswered in your mind, or were you curious about what might happen next for the characters? Write some of your questions here.

_____

_____

_____

_____

_____

_____

Work in groups or by yourself to prepare possible answers for some or all of the questions you have asked as well as those written below. When you finish your responses, share your ideas with the class.

- How has the treatment of whites and non-whites changed in Maycomb County courts over the years?
- Do juries still find innocent men guilty of crimes?
- Are there still prejudiced people in Maycomb? in other cities?
- Do non-whites want to be like whites? Do whites want to be like non-whites?
- Would Tom Robinson be found guilty today?
- Would someone known to be shiftless and a liar be able to get someone else convicted today?
- Would courts today demand that Mayella get a medical examination to prove she had been raped?
- Are girls in Maycomb still expected to act like ladies? Are they allowed to wear pants to school?
- If Scout were a child today, would she feel as if she were in a "pink-walled penitentiary?"
- How do people feel about having a "good family?"
- Do ladies in Maycomb still go to church every Sunday?
- How do girls speak to each other now? Do they speak differently to other people than they do to each other? Are girls looked down on for laughing in public? Do girls voice their opinions? Do girls ever use bad grammar?
- Is there still segregation in Maycomb? Do people of different races go to church together or to separate churches? Do black children go to different schools than white children? Are there still some children who do not go to school?
- Are children safe walking home from school at night?
- Do poor people live differently than people who have money?
- Are children able to play in the street?
- Do children still play games of "pretend?" Do they play the same games they played when Scout was a girl?
- Are there still dirt roads?
- How is clothing worn by children today different from the clothing in the book?
- Are parents still allowed to beat their children because they are theirs?
- Today, would a teacher be unhappy if a child could read before starting school?

Book Report Ideas

Reports on literature can be done in many ways. After reading *To Kill a Mockingbird*, use one of the following suggestions for your report or choose another of your own creation with your teacher's approval.

- **Make a bookworm** (page 33).

- **Write an autobiographical story**. The events and people in *To Kill a Mockingbird* are based on events and people Harper Lee knew as a child. No one person or event is exactly the same, but there were many similar people and events. When a book is based on the author's childhood, we say it is autobiographical because the author uses her own experiences as a basis for the ones in her story. Write your own autobiographical story based on your experiences.

- **Invent a game!** Jem, Dill, and Scout play games they have invented. In their games they often pretend to be other people. What kind of game would you invent? Would you pretend to be other people, as they do, or would you invent a board game, a game of sports, or a card game? Teach your game to your classmates.

- **Extend your reading**. Read another book about non-whites living in the United States, such as one from the bibliography of related reading (page 47). Write a report comparing and contrasting this book with *To Kill a Mockingbird*.

- **Design an advertising poster**. Using bright colors and your best imagination, make a poster to persuade others to read *To Kill a Mockingbird*. Choose something from the book which symbolizes it for you, and use that symbol as a logo for your poster.

- **Interview the author**. Together with a classmate prepare an interview with Harper Lee as you imagine it would go. For this you will have to research the author's life and interviews that have been done with her previously.

- **Change the point of view**. *To Kill a Mockingbird* was told from Scout's point of view. How might the story be different if it were told from the point of view of Atticus? Jem? Walter Cunningham? Tom Robinson? Calpurnia?

- **Write a poem**. Write your poem about a character or event in the novel.

- **Design a new dust jacket for the novel**. A dust jacket is the paper cover which fits over a hardback book. On the front of your dust jacket put the title, author's name, and publisher's name along with a picture of a scene or symbol from the story. On the back, write comments from classmates about it. Inside the front write a summary of it, and inside the back write a short biography of the author.

Research Ideas

Describe three things in *To Kill a Mockingbird* that you would like to learn more about.

1. _____

2. _____

3. _____

As you read the book, you may have encountered a part of the United States and a way of life you never knew because the story contains many events, procedures, ideas, beliefs, lifestyles, and even a writing style which may seem strange to you. Understanding these things will help to increase your understanding of the novel. It will also help you to appreciate Harper Lee's remarkable craft as a writer.

Work in groups or on your own to research one or more of the areas you named above or the areas named below. Share what you learn with the rest of the class in either a report or a project.

- the South
- plantation system
- segregation
- Dred Scott Case
- Underground Railroad
- slavery in America
- Great Depression
- Reconstruction
- the Crash of 1929
- World War I
- World War II
- Nazism
- the New Deal
- Ku Klux Klan
- rabies
- plants of Alabama
- hurricanes and tornadoes
- movies of the 1930s
- courtroom procedures
- prejudice and discrimination
- social class
- Disabilities Act
- propaganda
- Truman Capote
- "The Lottery" by Shirley Jackson

- the Civil War
- Industrial Revolution in America
- Jim Crow laws
- Alabama
- The Emancipation Proclamation
- southern cooking
- Franklin D. Roosevelt
- poverty in America
- Adolf Hitler
- Treaty of Versailles
- anti-Semitism
- white supremacists
- Social Security
- idioms
- Norman Rockwell paintings
- mockingbirds
- the 1930s
- history of radio
- jury system
- majority rule
- scapegoating
- mental illness
- Pulitzer Prize
- Bank Holiday of 1933

Culminating Activity

Reading a wonderful book like *To Kill a Mockingbird* deserves a celebration. What better way to do this than to participate in the old Alabama custom of "eating on the ground" (having a picnic), followed by viewing the movie version of the book, starring Gregory Peck. This movie is one of the best examples of how a great book can be turned into a great movie. After showing the film, discuss how closely it follows the novel. Does it show both plots? Why do the students think this is true? Is there any way in which they think the movie would be better?

For your picnic, follow this menu of typical Southern foods or choose ones of your own. If you wish, students can bring sack lunches instead and eat them outside or in the classroom before the movie begins.

> **Menu**
>
> vegetable munchies
>
> pea salad (page 23)
>
> potato salad
>
> fried chicken
>
> banana pudding with vanilla wafers (page 23)
>
> hush puppies (page 23)
>
> iced tea and lemonade

Activities and Displays

During your celebration, you can display the various work sheets, projects, and essays completed by the students. You can also have demonstrations of the following:

- Act out the meaning of idioms.
- Role-play.
- Demonstrate allusions.
- Discuss racial hatred and stereotyping.
- Share oral book reports.
- Draw and display maps of Maycomb.

- Create posters for the movie based on the book.
- Write movie reviews.
- Present author interviews (page 41).
- Play invented games (page 41).
- Share alternate points of view for the story (page 41).

Conversations

Work in size-appropriate groups to write and perform the conversation that might have occurred in one of the following situations.

- A few years after Tom Robinson's trial, Atticus goes to California to discuss defending a man accused of being involved in a lynching. Someone has told the accused lyncher of Atticus' part in Tom Robinson's defense, and he questions Atticus' ability to defend someone accused of taking part in a lynching.

- Mr. Underwood and Atticus discuss Mr. Underwood's editorial in the paper about Tom's trial and what the moral considerations are of Tom's conviction and his subsequent murder.

- As adults, Scout and Dill reminisce about their childhood escapades in trying to get Boo Radley to come out and the way in which their ideas of fun have changed.

- An adult Scout and Atticus, who is now an old man, discuss the trial of Tom Robinson and the social and economic changes they see as having taken place in the last thirty years in Maycomb.

- Calpurnia, now an old woman, and an adult Scout discuss the social and economic changes which have taken place for black people since the 1960s.

- Jem as an adult and Rev. Sykes, now an old man, discuss the Tom Robinson trial and what it meant to have Atticus defend Tom.

- Calpurnia and Rev. Sykes discuss the trial of Tom Robinson, its aftermath, and what social and economic changes they have seen since then.

- Helen Robinson and Calpurnia, both old women, discuss how Helen managed to raise four children alone after Tom Robinson was murdered and what it felt like to have to deal with such a tragedy.

- Scout visits Boo Radley in a nursing home where he is now an old man, and she attempts to discuss with him the times she, Dill, and Jem tried to make Boo come out. Miss Maudie is also present and tries to interpret for Boo since she has known him all her life. However, Boo himself begins to talk.

- As adults, Scout accompanies Dill on a trip to Kansas where Dill, now a writer, is doing research on a terrible crime that happened there. A family was killed in their farm house, and two men have been arrested for the crime. Together Scout and Dill interview people who knew the murdered family and ask them about the town where they grew up. The subject of Tom Robinson's trial arises.

- Atticus and his wife, before Jem and Scout are born, discuss what their children's futures may be like.

- Tom and Helen Robinson, before their children are born, discuss what their children's futures may be like.

- Tom Robinson gives his testimony in a present-day court.

Response

Explain the meanings of these quotations from *To Kill a Mockingbird:*

- "I just thought you'd like to know I can read. You got anything needs readin' I can do it . . ."
- "Your father does not know how to teach. You can have a seat now."
- "Reason I can't pass the first grade . . . is I've had to stay out ever' spring an' help Pa with the choppin', but there's another'n at the house now that's field size."
- I was on the verge of leavin'—I done my time for this year.
- "You never understand a person until you consider things from his point of view . . . until you climb into his skin and walk around in it."
- ". . . if Atticus Finch drank until he was drunk he wouldn't' be as hard as some men are at their best."
- "It must be some little kid's place—hides his things from the bigger folks. . . ."
- "You can't go around making caricatures of the neighbors."
- I looked down and found myself clutching a brown woolen blanket I was wearing around my shoulders squaw-fashion.
- He walked erratically, as if his right legs were shorter than his left legs. He reminded me of a car stuck in a sandbed.
- "Good evening Mrs. Dubose! You look like a picture this evening."
- Calpurnia motioned Jem and me to the end of the row and placed herself between us.
- "Put my bag in the front bedroom, Calpurnia . . . Jean Louise, stop scratching you head."
- " . . . you are not run-of-the-mill people, . . . you are the product of several generations' gentle breeding."
- I felt the starched walls of a pink cotton penitentiary closing in on me . . .
- "There's some men outside in the yard, they want you to come out."
- "Don't you remember me, Mr. Cunningham? I'm Jean Louise Finch. You brought us some hickory nuts one time, remember?"
- "Anything fit to say at the table's fit to say in front of Calpurnia. She knows what she means to this family."
- "You makin' fun o'me agin, Mr. Finch?"
- ". . . I felt right sorry for her, she seemed to try more'n the rest of 'em—"
- "This case is as simple as black and white."
- "Miss Jean Louise, stand up. Your father's passin'."
- ". . . They've done it before . . . and they'll do it again and when they do it—seems that only children weep. . . ."
- ". . . I think I'm beginning to understand something. I think I'm beginning to understand why Boo Radley stayed shut up in the house all this time. . . ."
- "Tom's dead."
- "I never wanta hear about that courthouse again, ever, ever, you hear me?"
- "If I hear one more peep outa my girl Helen about not bein' able to walk this road I'll have you in jail before sundown."
- "I can tell we're under the big oak because we're passin' through a cool spot."
- Our company shuffled and dragged his feet, as if wearing heavy shoes.
- The man was walking with the staccato steps of someone carrying a load too heavy for him.
- "He won't hurt these children again."

Objective Test and Essay

Matching: Match the descriptions of the characters with their names.

1. _____ Walter Cunningham
2. _____ Calpurnia
3. _____ Mayella Ewell
4. _____ Miss Maudie
5. _____ Mrs. DuBose
6. _____ Atticus
7. _____ Dill
8. _____ Judge Taylor
9. _____ Jem
10. _____ Rev. Sykes
11. _____ Scout
12. _____ Aunt Alexandria

a. takes the children into the courtroom
b. has a huge imagination
c. believes family is most important
d. fights for what he believes in
e. feels like she is in a pink-walled prison
f. wants his sister to act like a girl
g. overcomes her drug habit
h. is fair
i. is poor but proud
j. has been with the Finches all her life
k has her house burned down
l. does not know what love is

True or False: Answer true or false in the blanks below.

1. _____ Atticus succeeds in convicting Tom Robinson of beating and raping Mayella Ewell.

2. _____ Calpurnia wants the members of her church to be impressed with her care of the children.

3. _____ Mr. Cunningham is too ashamed to lynch Tom Robinson in front of the children.

4. _____ When Tom is killed, no one in town will help Helen and her children.

5. _____ Justice is served in Maycomb County when Tom is found guilty.

Short Answer: Write a brief response to each question in the space provided.

1. Who thinks Atticus should leave the teaching to her and why?

   _____

   _____

2. What do the children find in the knothole of the tree?

   _____

3. How does Jem react to Tom's killing? _____

   _____

4. Why does Dill spend summers in Maycomb?_____

   _____

5. When does Scout first see Boo Radley? _____

   _____

Essay: Choose one of these themes from *To Kill a Mockingbird* and write a persuasive essay telling why you think it is the most important one: stereotyping, justice, racial relationships, family, or parent-child relationships. Include in your essay your definition of the theme you have chosen.

Bibliography of Related Reading

Adler, David A. *The Number on My Grandfather's Arm*. UAHC Press, 1987.

Bray, Rosemary and Malcah Zeldis. *Martin Luther King*. Mulberry Books, 1997.

Cleaver, Vera and Bill Cleaver. *Where the Lilies Bloom*. Harper Trophy, 1989.

Frank, Anne. *The Diary of a Young Girl*. Bantam Books, 1993.

Greene, Bette. *Summer of My German Soldier*. Laurel Leaf, 1993.

Hinton, S. E. *The Outsiders*. Dell, 1989.

Houston, Jean and James D. *Farewell to Manzanar*. Bantam Books, 1974.

Keyes, Daniel. *Flowers for Algernon*. Bantam Books, 1984.

Marshall, James V. *Walkabout*. Sundance Publications, 1978.

Sebestyen, Ouida. *Words by Heart*. Bantam Books, 1996.

Taylor, Mildred D. *Roll of Thunder, Hear My Cry*. Bantam Books, 1976.

Taylor, Theodore. *The Cay*. Avon Books, The Hearst Corp., 1970.

Yep, Lawrence. *Child of the Owl*. Scholastic, 1990.

Yep, Lawrence. *Dragonwings*. HarperCollins, 1990.

Audio and Video Tapes

To Kill a Mockingbird (audio cassette). Audio Partners Publishing Corp., 1997.

To Kill a Mockingbird (video). MCA Bookservice, 1998.

Internet Sites

1933: http://www.YBI.COM/brink/author/1933/index.html

About Harper Lee: http://afroam.org/history/history.html

Black History Museum: http://www.afroam.org/history/history.html

Harper Lee and *To Kill a Mockingbird:* http://www.chebucto.ns.ca/Culture/HarperLee/

Encarta Advanced Search: http://encarta.com/find/default.asp

ESL Idiom Page: http://www.pacificnet.net/~sperling/idioms.cgi

Growing Up White in the South: http://library.advanced.org/12111/girl.html

Harper Lee Prizes Privacy: http://csmonitor.com/durable/1997/09/11/feat/feat.3.html

Literacy Education Online: http://leo.stcloud.msus.edu/acadwrite/conclude.html

Monroe County Heritage Museums: http://www.tokillamockingbird.com./

The Five-Paragraph Essay: http://members.aol.com/AACTchAndy/edu/essayform.html

The Scottsboro Boys: http://www.afroam.org/history/scott/scotts.html

A special thanks to Leslie McLeod of Alabama for her recipe for Alabama hush puppies.

Answer Key

Page 10
1. Accept appropriate responses.
2. Responses may include such things as: "the summer Dill came to us"; main residential street in county seat in Maycomb, Alabama; an old town.
3. Atticus Finch, a lawyer, is their father. Their mother is dead.
4. Responses may include such things as: small; seven years old; can read; "I'm little but I'm old," he says about himself; lives in Meridian, Mississippi; won a beautiful baby contest; has seen the movie *Dracula;* wears shorts that button to his shirt; has snow-white hair and blue eyes; laughs a lot; tells stories.
5. The teacher is from out of town and does not realize that the Cunninghams are poor but proud and should not be embarrassed by being reminded of their poverty in public.
6. They are confused and afraid at first, but then they decide to keep the things until they find out who has left them.
7. They dislike the Radleys because they do not go to church, and they keep to themselves with their doors and shutters closed. It is rumored that Boo once stabbed his mother.
8. It is Jem's idea of someone who has died and cannot get to heaven, so he wallows around on lonesome roads, and a person can walk right through him. Jem believes that if you do so, when you die you will be a hot steam, too, sucking people's breath right out of them.
9. She is a neighbor who allows the children to play on her lawn, eat her scuppernongs, and explore her property. She is a widow who wears overalls to work in her flower beds and then bathes and sits on her porch from which she observes everything that happens on the street.
10. Accept appropriate responses.

Page 17
1. Accept appropriate responses.
2. He wants to try to peek in the window to see Boo.
3. His pants are neatly mended and hung on the fence.
4. Boo has placed it there without her being aware of it.
5. Tom is a black man from Calpurnia's church whom Atticus has been named to defend against the charge of raping a white woman.
6. He feels they should be answered honestly and respected just as adult questions would be. Examples will vary.
7. Atticus says this because mockingbirds cause no harm and do nothing except give pleasure and joy to people with their singing. Responses as to Atticus' meaning will vary; accept all reasonable responses.
8. She recognizes the dog has rabies, calls Atticus to come home, urges the children into the house with orders to stay there, and runs to alert the neighbors that a mad dog is in the street.
9. He believes she is courageous because she decides she is going to overcome her addiction to drugs before she dies, and she does.
10. Accept appropriate responses.

Page 22
1. Accept appropriate responses.
2. She makes them scrub much more than usual and really dress up in nice clothes.
3. Calpurnia teaches him a page of the Bible every day, and he also reads from Blackstone's Commentaries.
4. Aunt Alexandria is preoccupied with family background and appearances.
5. Dill is hiding there because, as he says, he has escaped from his new stepfather who beats and starves him.
6. Mr. Levy tells them that he sold them the sheets they are wearing. He shames them.
7. He is waiting for the men who were going to try to take Tom Robinson, and he wants to get the men to go home. When they see the children, Jem refuses to go, and Scout kicks one of the men and shames Mr. Cunningham. They finally leave.
8. He says they are a mob and like a bunch of animals because when they get together they act like animals until they are in front of the children.
9. The children go to the balcony with Rev. Sykes.
10. Accept appropriate responses.

Page 26
1. Hamlet
2. Mary I (Mary Tudor)
3. Nazi Germany
4. Benito Mussolini
5. Queen Elizabeth I
6. Thomas Alva Edison
7. Dr. Martin Luther King, Jr.
8. Franklin Delano Roosevelt
9. Bible
10. Bible
11. Adolf Hitler
12. Romeo and Juliet

Page 27
1. Accept appropriate responses.
2. She does not like him or understand him, and she is afraid he is going to do to her what she thinks he has done to her father, which is to make fun of her.
3. She asks him what he means.
4. She was beaten by someone left-handed, because most of her injuries were on the right side of her face. Tom Robinson's left hand is crippled, and he could not use it for anything.
5. He says he helped her for free, because he felt sorry for her. At this place and time, for a black man to feel sorry for a white woman was to put himself in a position above her, and that was unacceptable.
6. When Dill takes a drink of the bottle he carries in a sack, Dill finds it is just cola, not whiskey as everyone thinks.
7. When Calpurnia tells him the children were missing, he knows they were in the courtroom.
8. He cries, knowing the verdict is not right. He is angry and does not understand how the jury could have done that.
9. He wipes his face with a handkerchief, and when Ewell asks him if he is afraid to fight, he answers, "No, too old."
10. Accept appropriate responses.

Page 32
1. Accept appropriate responses.
2. They forget about the case quickly. Also, Scout believes that Maycomb's children are instructed not to talk about the case in front of Scout and Jem because they are not to blame for their father's actions (people generally believing that Atticus was wrong to defend Tom Robinson).
3. He walks Helen home from work, stops at the Ewell's house, and tells them that if they ever bother Helen again, he will have them thrown in jail. When they do, he threatens them again, and they leave Helen alone.
4. Scout plays a ham.
5. Scout spends her money on the House of Horrors as well as buying some divinity and some taffy.
6. She cannot change because it is dark, and she cannot see to put on her dress.
7. Jem and Scout hear someone and start running. Someone grabs Scout, and she can hear his heavy breathing and smell whiskey. Then suddenly he is flung away by someone else, and she looks to see someone carrying Jem under the street light. Jem's arm is broken, and he is knocked unconscious.
8. Bob Ewell is found, and he is dead.
9. She is telling Mr. Heck Tate about how a stranger saved her and Jem, when she looks over into the corner and sees Boo. She recognizes him as the person she had seen carrying Jem under the street light.
10. Accept appropriate responses.

Page 45
Responses will vary. Accept all sound and well-supported meanings.

Page 46
Matching
1. i
2. j
3. l
4. k
5. g
6. d
7. b
8. h
9. f
10. a
11. e
12. c

True or False
1. false
2. true
3. true
4. false
5. false

Short Answer
1. Miss Caroline thinks the teaching should be left to her because she believes Atticus is unqualified to teach and will do damage to Scout's learning.
2. They find gum, pennies, and a watch.
3. Jem is very upset and does not want to talk about it.
4. Dill's parents are divorced, and he stays with his aunt when school is out for the summer.
5. Scout first sees Boo Radley when he carries Jem under the streetlight.

Essay: Accept appropriate responses.